Pathways

to Enrollment Growth and Retention for Catholic School Leaders

Authors

Adam J. Dufault
Interim Superintendent, Archdiocese of Denver
Denver, Colorado

Annette Marie Jones, Ed.S.
Assistant Director of Leadership Development
National Catholic Educational Association (NCEA)
Arlington, Virginia

Contributors

Kevin D. Kijewski, J.D. (Foreword)
Maria Ippolito

Reviewers

Kevin D. Kijewski, J.D.

NCEA.
National Catholic Educational Association

www.NCEA.org

ISBN: 978-1-55833-663-6
Part Number: ADM-70-1591

TABLE of Contents

FOREWORD

atholic schools are not just places that promote academic excellence and environments conducive to learning; they are also sacred spaces that educate our children to be a new generation of saints in this life and the next. The value of Catholic education is clearly evident for those of us that work in leadership. However, the problem is that a growing number of prospective students and families are not aware of the full value and potential of what our schools have to offer. Adam Dufault and Annette Jones address this problem head-on in this book and offer practical, turn-key strategies to help Catholic school leaders increase enrollment.

This book provides a valuable window on enrollment growth strategies and covers the necessary components, from creating appealing value propositions for prospective families to best practices for promoting retention of existing students. The techniques covered in this book will help Catholic schools prioritize highly effective marketing efforts that will yield enrollment growth. With the internet, social media, smartphones and tablet computers playing a larger role in our daily lives, the authors show how schools may easily leverage social media to target a broad prospective market of families.

The challenges in growing our Catholic schools are both difficult and interesting. People are working on them with enthusiasm, tenacity and dedication to share the good news about the efficacy of our schools. In this new age of information interconnectivity and very discerning parents, it is necessary to provide Catholic school leaders with state-of-the-art strategies and guidance to effectively recruit and retain families. This book is a good step in that direction.

Kevin D. Kijewski, J.D.
Superintendent of Catholic Schools
Archdiocese of Detroit

INTRODUCTION

"Welcome to the best-kept secret in town!" a parent proudly said to me, with a big smile. I (Adam) had just started as the principal of a Catholic school, and this phrase summed up the philosophy of enrollment growth that had led to a large number of available seats. This school, like so many others, had taken an ineffective approach to marketing and enrollment management. Unfortunately, this school was not alone, as the troubling statistics demonstrate.

Catholic school enrollment peaked in the 1960s. Those were the halcyon days of Catholic education, when schools were full—often too full—and the hard-working priests and sisters of many orders provided excellent instruction at impossibly low tuitions. Today, it is no secret that many of our schools are struggling with lower enrollments, and reports of school closures are all too common. Yet, our schools have never been needed more than they are in this day and age. Cardinal Timothy Dolan of New York observed, "Without a doubt Catholic schools are an unquestioned success in every way: spiritually, academically and communally. More to the point, the graduates they produce emerge as lifelong practitioners of their faith. These Catholic graduates have been, are and will be our leaders in church and society." [Dolan, Cardinal Timothy M. "The Catholic Schools We Need." *America* Magazine. September 13, 2010.]

What can we do about this trend? The answer is to change the mindset of school leaders. We cannot be content any longer with being a well-kept secret. We should be screaming the good news of Catholic education from every rooftop in town! How do we accomplish this? There are many lessons and parallels to the business world that can help us respond to the challenges of enrollment growth efficiently and effectively. The answer is through the proper marketing and promotion of our schools.

Marketing takes two distinct yet interconnected pathways. The first is retention, that is, keeping the families that have enrolled in your Catholic school as part of your school community for as long as possible. After all, if you can keep the students that you have, you don't have to work as hard to find new ones. Retention can be misunderstood as appeasement, that is, keeping the families happy at all costs, but that is not the case. Good retention strategies keep families feeling connected, and those bonds lead to the word of mouth that is so critical in developing a school's reputation. Recruitment, then, can focus on reaching out to bring new families into the school and raising the profile of the school in a community. If no one knows where your school is or why it exists in the first place, no one is going to click on your website or drop off their children at your door.

In this book, we will share our experiences as Catholic school leaders and provide other principals with easy ideas and suggestions for both retention and recruitment. Many other excellent books and workshops have tackled the fundamentals of enrollment management, so we will not attempt to re-create them. (We would be happy to recommend some excellent resources, if that is what you need). Instead, we present ideas, from two former principals to all current principals, in a spirit of collegiality rooted in the desire to share the Gospel message with all children and families.

CHAPTER 1
Value Proposition

Before exploring any strategies, we first must be clear on the purpose of our schools. Several years ago, the Big Shoulders Fund in Chicago developed a strategy to engage schools in a process of defining their value propositions. Maria Ippolito of the Big Shoulders Fund and a consultant with Partners in Mission explains this concept:

> When we talk about marketing in our schools, we tend to focus on *things*, like brochures, billboards and branding. We want the shiny new logo and the perfectly designed viewbook. No doubt, these elements are key components of any marketing campaign, but before you can embark on the branding process, you need to define your value proposition.

"Value proposition" can feel like an intimidating term, but really it is quite simple. It is the answer to these questions: *What makes your school unique? What makes your school special? What are the key differentiators that make your school stand out from the competition?* **At the most basic level, your value proposition answers the question, "Why would someone (spend money to) send *their* child to *your* school?"** Answering this question is the most important thing you can do when creating your marketing plan. You need to come back to the question over and over again and answer it multiple times to multiple audiences. It is the central component in any marketing plan.

It's important to keep in mind that, for years, "Catholic and safe" were the compelling key differentiators from the FREE competition. Parents no longer view this as being persuasive enough. "Catholic and safe" are inherent elements of your school's value proposition and core messages, but we need to tell them more.

Our value proposition must also delve into the **why** rather than just the **what**. While it is okay to list all the wonderful programs that your school offers, it becomes truly compelling when you explain **why** you offer these programs and the **outcomes** of such programs. In other words, a laundry list of after school clubs is okay, but an even better approach is to go beyond the list and explain that after school programs offer an enhancement to the daily curriculum and build well-rounded children who develop leadership skills and succeed in high school and beyond. Parents will care that you offer robust enrichment programs, but they will choose your school once they understand why you offer them and the outcomes for students who participate in them. Ultimately they need to know—from you—why all of the "whats" are so important for **their** children.

Remember to keep it simple. Think of maybe the five to seven key elements that make your school special. Spell them out in concise core messages. Think of the ways that you'll "prove them," and the communication vehicles that will allow you to share these messages. Then read the result—is this really different than any school? Different than the neighboring public school? Different than the neighboring Catholic school? If not, start over and improve the story, or, in some cases, work to improve the product. Once you've done this, you have a well-rounded value proposition from which you can build your entire marketing plan.

Pathway to Creating a Value Proposition

1. Consider your target audience (typically a parent of a young child). What are their needs? Concerns? What is the problem you can solve for them?

2. When considering your target audience, think about the language that is most appealing to them. Does a parent really understand educational language?

3. Your value proposition must be genuine. For example, you cannot call yourself a STEM school if you only offer basic science and math courses.

4. You'll need to prove it and think through the most compelling ways to "prove" your value. Some aspiration is fine, but all aspiration isn't credible.

5. Consider including testimonial statements as proof for most, if not all, of the core messages. Families value hearing validation from multiple sources.

6. Pictures are incredibly powerful in all marketing materials, but they must be high quality. A low-quality, grainy image doesn't have nearly the same impact as a clear image and, in fact, it sends a negative message. Also, large group shots typically don't have the same impact as a more focused image including one or only several students. Consider hiring a professional photographer.

7. Social media is a powerful place to tell your story, so please include that in your communications of the value proposition. Your website is a vehicle to communicate your value proposition, but increasingly social media is the way to actually engage in a dialogue and relationship with potential and current families.

8. Your value proposition is the most essential component of your marketing plan. It is your DNA and your brand in word form. Once your value proposition is communicated regularly and compellingly to your audience, it will empower parents to tell your story, and it will allow them to understand the true value of a Catholic education. Once they have those tools, your word of mouth marketing will have the fuel it needs to be successful, and ultimately, your enrollment will grow.

CHAPTER 2
Branding Your School

What do you think of when you see a large, yellow "M" on a sign? Hungry? Great fries? How about a green mermaid face? Feel the need for a little extra caffeine? These symbols are examples of excellent branding. The companies, McDonald's and Starbucks, have done such a great job developing identities that you recognize them from a single letter or image in a certain color. There is a powerful lesson in this concept. How recognizable are your school's logos and images? Do people think of your school when they see a certain color or symbol? Just like any business with ambitions for growth, our Catholic schools also need to have brand identification that is clear, crisp, and easily identifiable. The school's brand must be a visual summary of the value proposition.

Once, when Catholic schools were booming, the brand was easy to identify. Just a look at Sister in her habit told you what was happening inside the building. In those years, Sister was, in a sense, a symbol of the brand of Catholic education. Parents knew exactly what the school would provide in an instant. The reputation that developed was that of a school providing an outstanding, rigorous education.

Few schools have good, consistent branding or powerful, visual representations of their value propositions. It is more common for the school logo to be a jumble of symbols next to a cross with too many colors. To be effective, a logo must be carefully designed, aligned to the story that the school wants to tell about itself and guarded as nearly sacrosanct in its usage.

One of the best Catholic school logos can be found at St. Matthias School in Chicago, Illinois. Here is the logo:

Though it appears simple, the school is actually saying a lot about itself in this image. St. Matthias is located in a neighborhood called Lincoln Square, and this is apparent in the square design of the insignia. The school advertises itself as being located in the heart of Lincoln Square, so all arrows are pointing toward the center. The school is also well known for its diversity—economic, demographic and student ability—and so the arrows are in four different colors. Finally, the negative space in the logo forms a cross, emphasizing the school's

Catholicity. St. Matthias adapts this logo for various school events, making the appearance consistent and instantly recognizable. For example, here is an ingenious use of the logo for the school's annual Christmas tree sale:

St. Matthias SCHOOL **Tree Lot**

As you can see, the color scheme, the line weight, the typeface and the arrow theme are all preserved. This ensures that the connection to the school is readily apparent and visible.

Schools need to have a brand. They need an easily identifiable symbol that shows the world what they are and what they stand for. Like St Matthias, schools should use their symbols everywhere. The more times it is seen, the more easily the community at large makes the association between the symbol and what it represents.

In order to preserve the integrity of the school's brand, the logo must be guarded carefully. It needs to be used consistently on all official school items, like t-shirts, posters, signs and letterheads. Policies may need to be written, such as this one:

> The school name and logos are property of St. Matthias Parish. Persons may not use the St. Matthias School name or logo on printed materials without written consent from the principal. Any t-shirts, sweatshirts or other items featuring the school's name or logo must be pre-approved by the school principal. This includes articles for sports teams, parent organizations and events. *St. Matthias Family Handbook, 2013-14.*

Though this policy may seem strict, it preserves the image of the school.

Similarly, schools may want to create a style guide that extends beyond the logo. Choosing one font for all school communication, one design for the letterhead and a color scheme for all communication further solidifies the brand. These rules must be written down and shared with all in a position to communicate for the school.

To summarize, your school's brand is your face to the broader community. It is a symbol that represents your value proposition and communicates something about you. With some creativity, your school's brand can be iconic and easily build recognition in the community.

Pathway to Creating a Brand

1. Begin with a survey of parents, teachers, students and other major stakeholders.

2. Identify the ideas and the unique features of your school that make it stand out from all others.

3. Find a way to visually represent those ideas. You might consult a parent or parishioner with a background in graphic design.

4. Unveil the new logo with much fanfare and publicize it far and wide.

5. Make sure that the new logo is used on all uniforms, letterhead, websites, email communication, etc. It may even be a good idea to have vinyl logos created so that you can apply them to some doors and windows around your building.

CHAPTER 3
Online Opportunities

Think about how you find activities and services today. For example, if you feel like heading out to an Italian restaurant, how do you find one near you? Most likely, you pull out your smartphone and Google it. So does the current generation of parents who are looking for schools for their children.

The parents of today are the "digital natives," that is, the children who were born shortly after the internet became ubiquitous. Online life is normal to these parents, and Catholic schools need to be sure they are speaking to this generation.

Unfortunately, that still isn't happening. I (Adam) recently learned about a school that had nearly $1,000 in its budget earmarked for advertising in the Yellow Pages. No offense to the good folks at the phone company, but I can't remember the last time I looked at the Yellow Pages as anything other than a doorstop. Today's parents are not thinking about schools and letting their fingers do the walking. Instead, they are Googling. Schools need to ensure that they are in that space.

Social Media

Your school needs to be on social media NOW. No question about it—social media has quickly become one of the primary means of communication and information sharing in the United States. Your school should take advantage of all that Facebook and Twitter can offer.

Setting up the accounts is easy and free. The first step, though, is choosing someone to serve as your school's point person on social media communication. This can be a parent, a teacher, an administrator or a volunteer, but whoever it is must have a school-based email address, and the username and password must be shared with the school principal and pastor. This ensures that the accounts do not become the personal property of any one person and it allows for easy editing if need be. Your school should also have a protocol in place for receiving administrative approval for all posts and for following your school or diocesan policies on photo sharing.

Facebook is a great place to start. Your school will want to develop a page and ensure that contact information, school descriptions and photos are present. Facebook posts can showcase special events at your school, facts about the value of Catholic education and photos of daily life in your school. Perhaps the best feature of Facebook is the ability to boost posts and to target ads. Though there is a cost to use this service, it is relatively inexpensive and certainly much cheaper than any outdated print ad format. By boosting posts and targeting ads, you can increase the number of people who see your posts. You can even have Facebook share your ad with very specific demographics, say, young mothers living in the ZIP codes closest to your school.

Twitter is also very easy to set up. The trick to Twitter is that the number of characters that you may use is limited. So, creativity comes into play—how to say a lot with very little. Simply create a handle, or username, for your school that is descriptive about your name and location. For example, the Archdiocese of Denver's Office of Catholic Schools tweets as @ DenCathSchools. The key to being an effective Twitter user is frequency. You should attempt to post on Twitter at least three times a week. That way, you will be able to build a following and show up in the feeds of users.

Websites

Almost all schools have a website. Those few that do not are missing a significant opportunity to share themselves with the world. Websites do not have to be complicated or all that difficult to build or to maintain. If your school does not have one, the easiest way to create one is to investigate a service such as Squarespace (www.squarespace.com). This site allows you to create a simple, easily maintained web presence for a reasonable cost. Some schools may try to save money by creating a web presence that is a page off of the parish website. Unfortunately, this does not help a school stand out and will not drive traffic to the site.

Once a school has established a website, content must be added that reaches your intended audience. Most schools must decide between using their website as a tool to recruit new families or as a way of communicating with current families. Our recommendation is for the first option. Communication with current families can be easily managed through a Student Information System, through email blasts, and through social media. Your school website is your chance to share your story with the world. The home page must feature the school's logo, contact information, location, a compelling photo or photo scroll and information about the grade levels served. Additional pages should highlight the academic program, the staff and administration, admissions information, a school calendar, special programming for students and information about donating. Bright, colorful photos should be included throughout. You should use a color scheme and font that match your branding and ensure that all pages have a similar feel to them.

If you already have a school website, you need to make sure that it is being reviewed and updated frequently, at least on a weekly basis. Stale websites, such as those that still show the details of the Christmas play in March, can send the same signal as a dirty entryway or a phone that keeps ringing with no one answering. Keep in mind your intended audience and the image you would like to present.

Once you have established a good website, you might consider working with a service to improve your search engine optimization. This plan is simply increasing the likelihood that your school's website appears near the top of online search returns. For example, St. Catherine Laboure School in Glenview, Illinois, worked with a parent who specializes in search engine optimization to create microsites, small one-page websites that improve search results. The site, glenviewpreschool.com, was created because this was a common search term in the school's area. When parents enter "Glenview preschool" into Google, the microsite is at or near the top of the search return list. The small, one-page site provides information about the preschool program at the school and then links the parent to the main school website. Search engine optimization is not a costly process, and it will help to improve your visibility online.

Online Reviews

In industries that are dependent on good service and reputation, such as restaurants and hotels, online reviews are critical. Review sites are monitored, and reviews are responded to quickly. Schools need to be in this space, too. Reviews are how your school will be judged. Sites such as Facebook, Google and GreatSchools.com can be used to share the good news of your school. It would be a good idea to encourage families to post reviews online. You can even bring Chromebooks or iPads to a school advisory board meeting and spend the first 15 minutes of the meeting posting reviews. Unfortunately, there will be times when negative reviews are posted. It is a fact of life that your school will never please everyone, and some people will take it out on you online. The best defense against negative reviews is not legal action or anger. It is simply drowning out the bad reviews with good ones. Keep things positive and encourage as many satisfied parents as you can to post their experience of your school.

Photos

The old cliche, "A picture tells a thousand words," could not be more true in the world of school websites. Good photos and videos are an essential component of your web presence, so much so that a text-only website is extremely hard to find. Photos and videos give potential parents a glimpse into your school, helping them to visualize what having their child in your school might look like. For that reason, it is important that your photos focus on action shots, that is, students doing something academic, athletic, spiritual or engaging.

Videos

If a picture is worth a thousand words, then a well-produced video is easily good for ten thousand. Videos are a fantastic way to help prospective parents envision their families at your school. Good videos should be short—no more than three to five minutes long—with every shot used well-considered. Prospective families want to see your school living and breathing. They are thinking, "What happens in your building? Can I picture my child there, too?" A good video must capture this. A good strategy is to have a videographer record activity in your school on any given day. Images of students learning, completing assignments, playing at recess, walking down the hallway, at Mass, saying prayers, on the playground, in art class or walking into the building convey powerful messages. Set these images to music (be sure to secure the copyright permission if needed) and let the story unfold. The adult presence should be kept to a minimum. A long speech by a principal citing statistics or accolades does not make for compelling viewing, although a short, minimalist voice-over can be effective. Your students tell your school's story—let them shine.

Pathway for Creating Online Opportunities

1. Develop an online presence/social media committee.

2. Review your website. Who is your audience? How does it look?

3. Review your social media presence.

4. Create social media accounts if needed.

5. Share your social media accounts far and wide. Publicize them in bulletins and newsletters. Have a school-wide contest to see if you can reach a certain threshold of "likes" or "followers." For example, have an ice cream party if the school reaches 300 likes on Facebook in two months.

6. Link your school's accounts to social media accounts from your diocesan Office of Catholic Schools. Share their posts and they will share yours, thereby greatly increasing your reach.

7. Post reviews of your school and encourage parents to write reviews.

8. Consider Google search optimization.

9. Tell your story! Use photos as much as possible.

10. Develop a plan for maintaining your website and accounts each week. Never let either become stale!

11. Create a school video to post on your website and social media accounts.

CHAPTER 4
Marketing via Word of Mouth

The parking lot, the football stadium and the vestibule after Mass are powerful places. Our stakeholders, such as parents, prospective parents, grandparents, community members and parishioners, gather and share the latest news and information about our schools. Even though we may not know what messages are exchanged in these places, as Catholic school leaders, we can listen, educate and assist with the information that is circulated.

Most importantly, we must listen with an open mind and heart. We need to think of how to position ourselves to hear and acknowledge the positive and negative messages that are circulated. One great strategy for the parking lot is to arrive at least 15 minutes prior to dismissal and move among the groups of parents—rain or shine! Often, parents may have a "quick question" that can be immediately and accurately answered. Parents often appreciate the leader's visibility and responsiveness to their questions, suggestions and concerns. Also, the habit of carrying a cell phone is a great practice for communication with the school office and as a place to jot notes for follow-up with parents. Effective leaders consistently follow up with parents within 24 hours of a conversation.

Secondly, our goal is to educate our stakeholders. As school leaders, we serve as the cornerstone for marketing efforts. What do we want our stakeholders to know? Some essential topics come to mind, such as the mission and vision of our school, the history of the school, the practices of missionary discipleship, the academic excellence and supporting data, the leadership and professionalism of the staff and the financial picture of the institution. One best practice is to write a paragraph about each topic area, memorize the key points and utilize the information as "elevator speeches" when opportunities arise to share information about these topics as they pertain to your school.

How do elevator speeches translate into practice? For example, following a parent's question in the parking lot, I (Annette) would answer their question, ask about their children and then share one news item about the school. I have found that these "news items" cover a majority of audiences and situations. For anything outside of these areas, I would share limited information, but soon after reflect on the topic and develop another elevator speech. Overall, consistent verbal messaging is essential from the leader of the school. By rotating the "news items," parents will feel "in the know" and can pass accurate information to their peers, colleagues and neighbors.

Of course, principals cannot be in all places at all times. We need assistance from our colleagues and selected parents and community members. Develop a marketing team of eight to ten people who can share and report back what is happening in the communication pipeline, especially during dismissal, at sporting events and after Mass. Select marketing members who have different touch points in the school, parish and community, so the outgoing and incoming information is broad based.

Here is an example of effectively using the communication pipeline. During the summer, a majority of the elementary school moms belonged to one local swimming pool. Since I (Annette) wasn't a member, nor interested in modeling a swimsuit in front of the school community, I asked two reliable marketing moms to share the pool topics with me. By the way, the pipeline works both ways as I shared accurate information through the marketing moms to the pool moms. I touched base with the marketing moms in mid-June, mid-July and mid-August.

As I heard the topics, I addressed any questions or concerns, especially in the areas of staffing and curriculum, in the June and July parent newsletters. If I heard topics at the end of the summer or multiple times during the summer, I addressed the topics during the Back-to-School Night presentations. Regardless of how I learned the information, I believe that parents felt "heard" and their questions and concerns were addressed in a timely manner.

Pathway for Marketing via Word of Mouth

1. Listen with an open mind and heart.

2. Seize opportunities for verbal communication.

3. Use the parking lot, sporting events, vestibule after Mass and other gathering places to communicate with stakeholders.

4. Carry and use a cell phone for follow-up notes.

5. Develop elevator speeches about key topics relating to the school.

6. Create and coach a small marketing team to assist with the communication pipeline.

7. Prepare newsletters that answer questions and concerns from stakeholders.

CHAPTER 5
School Tours for Prospective Families

The school tour is one of the most important aspects in the marketing and admission process. Many educators and leaders believe that the principal is solely responsible for the marketing of the school. However, the reality is that every person affiliated with the school—teachers, staff members, students, parents, parishioners—are all marketers of the school. Each one of us has an extremely significant role in telling our story and inspiring others to become members of our school community.

Let's reflect: How did you become involved in your school community? What do you like the most about your school community? What would you share in terms of spirituality, academics and the top three news items with a prospective family?

The first step for a tour begins with the intake phone call or intake form via the website. This basic intake form contains information about the names of the parents, the family's home address, the names and grades of the children and their previous school. Principals need to do their homework! Read about their previous school so you can compare and contrast the selling points of that school and your school. In addition, information about the prospective family's previous school can offer insight into their values in selecting a school.

Principals should be the primary tour guides. However, in special circumstances like open houses, board members or students may accompany, or perhaps lead, a tour. Best practice is to offer training to parents and board members prior to an open house event and to provide the tour route, talking points and special information about the school and teachers. Encourage the tour guides to arrive at least 15 minutes early for any last minute questions or explanations.

Students who serve as school ambassadors should also receive training prior to an open house. A training session should coach students on making formal introductions and answering parents' questions about spirituality, academics and extracurricular activities. Also, teach students how to respond to difficult questions and how to open the conversation to involve the adult tour guide. I recommend that a student is paired with an adult guide on school tours.

After a warm greeting and introduction, ask the parents and each child, "What would you like to see on the tour?" Nothing like receiving a list of interests before you begin! Point out these areas in your school during the tour! Show your school pride and be honest and careful with all responses. For example, if you do not have a drama club, then simply state that drama is not offered as an extracurricular activity. Be careful with questions regarding comparisons to other Catholic schools. Usually, redirecting the parents to the websites is a tactful solution. Remember that parents are not only listening to your answers as a professional leader, they are also observing your affective skills, such as listening skills, integrity, attentiveness, warmth and rapport with their children.

Teachers and staff members are essential parts of the marketing process. As soon as a tour is scheduled, communicate the date and time with the teachers and staff members, so they have a "heads up" to tidy the classrooms or to update a bulletin board. Most importantly, teachers and staff members need to be prepared with talking points in case they are introduced to the prospective family on the tour. Each semester, principals should review formal introductions, emphasizing good eye contact, a warm smile and firm handshake with all guests at a faculty meeting.

If a teacher is seated at his or her desk without students in the classroom, then he or she should walk to the door to greet the family. If a teacher is in the middle of a lesson, then the teacher should follow the principal's lead. If the teacher is in the middle of a lesson, but a prospective child is entering that grade level, the principal should assist with the lesson, so the prospective parents can meet and talk briefly with the teacher. Regardless of the circumstances, all teachers and staff members should be prepared for formal introductions and to share a spirituality point (curriculum, sacrament, retreat, etc.), academic point (curriculum, special program, etc.) and three upcoming events (classroom, grade level, team, school-wide event or program). At a faculty meeting, the principal should lead a practice session so teachers can role-play their answers to prospective parents.

On a tour, prospective parents should expect appropriate engagement with the students in our schools. Best practice in marketing means reminding students about formal introductions, eye contact and manners. In addition, teachers should discuss possible questions that prospective parents may ask them about the school, such as favorite classes, activities or sports.

The principal, in conjunction with the school advisory board, should develop an admission policy, timeline and systematic admission process for each prospective student. An admission policy may include, but is not limited to, the acceptance order of students, required documentation, completed and signed application, application deposit, medical requirements, types of assessments and writing samples. The office staff must ensure that all applications are date stamped. The prospective student's records must be transferred to the school, reviewed thoroughly by the principal and discussed with the teachers prior to the student's admission to the school.

The process of building a relationship with a family begins with the first hello and the handshake. As decisions are finalized about admissions, prospective parents expect honesty from the school personnel. Please share difficult information, such as the fact that one child of three will be on a waiting list, with kindness and in a gentle tone. After all, our goal is to help our prospective families to become happy, engaged families who are actively recruiting families to our schools.

Pathway for School Tours

1. Reflect on your involvement in the school. What do you enjoy about the school? What are the challenges? What are spiritual, academic and upcoming events and activities?

2. Create an intake form for phone calls, in-person and website requests for tours.

3. Share the dates and times of tours with the teachers. If available, include the names and grade levels of the prospective students as well.

4. Do your homework about the previous school of a prospective family. Be prepared to know your schools comparative strengths and challenges.

5. Provide training for adults or students who will assist with school tours.

6. Provide a tour route, talking points and special information about the school or teachers to the tour guides.

7. Discuss formal introductions, procedures when a tour arrives at the classroom and talking points with a prospective family.

8. Ask prospective parents and students what they would like to see on the school tour.

9. Keep in mind that prospective parents want a Catholic school leader who is faith-filled, has professional knowledge and possesses affective skills.

CHAPTER 6
Spiritual Events for Community Engagement

The Tradition of the Family Groups Program

At St. Louis de Montfort Catholic School, I (Annette) believe that one special tradition for all students was the Family Groups Program. Family Groups is a way to organize the students so that students get to know, work with and have fun with students at various grade levels.

Each fall, a Family Group committee of teachers and staff members divides the school staff into pairs. One practical suggestion is to match a teacher of younger students with a teacher of older students. In addition, the special area teachers are assigned as third members of a teacher pair, so they could become substitutes if a paired teacher is absent from a Family Group activity.

The Family Groups program develops the leadership skills of all students, especially the junior high students. Our teachers intentionally divide these students by considering their friendships, boy/girl ratios, and temperament of the junior high students. After the junior high students are placed into groups with their teacher pairs, then the remaining students are assigned to a Family Group. After constructing the groups, the committee shares the list with all members of the staff and requests their input as it is possible to overlook special circumstances across an entire student body.

When the lists are finalized, the committee invites the teachers to brainstorm the names and colors for their Family Group. For example, teachers would select a patron saint and one color to identify their Family Group. Next, the committee solicits input for a mixture of spiritual, academic, and fun activities to enjoy during the six to eight Family Groups meetings throughout the year. Through this interactive Family Groups program, teachers and administrators have witnessed leadership skills, compassion, sensitivity, new friendships, and improved leadership and communication skills.

Calendar of Activities

September: Meet and Greet Family Groups. Do introductions and a "get to know you game."

October: Attend Mass in Family Groups. Create prayer cards for first responders.

November: Service Project. Each student brings in present for the needy family. Create cards and gift boxes for soldiers.

December: Students read a Christmas story and write Christmas cards for nursing home residents.

January: Collect socks, hats and mittens for a local charity. Students learn about a different country and present information to another Family Group.

February: Engage in a school-wide service project for Catholic Schools Week. Students can participate in a "coin war" to raise money for board games, coloring books, markers, etc. for a Children's Hospital.

March: Washing of the Hands: Eighth grade leaders lead a simple prayer service and wash the hands of the students in their group. Following Washing of the Hands, students fill plastic Easter eggs for the parish Easter egg hunt. Encourage the junior high students to plan the prayers, songs, and instrumental music for the prayer service.

April: Students play board games and card games in Family Groups. The committee can also arrange a school-wide bingo game.

May: The annual Staff vs. 8th Grade Volleyball Game is scheduled on the morning of Field Day. Students sit in Family Groups and cheer for their favorite team.

Pathway for the Creation of Family Groups

1. Brainstorm activities for Family Groups as a staff. Keep in mind spiritual, academic, social, cultural, and service-related activities.

2. Form a small committee (about six people) to create a master calendar of Family Group activities.

3. Determine which staff members are responsible for planning and implementing each event.

4. Divide students into Family Groups. For example, assign two or more students per grade level to create each family group.

5. Schedule a meeting with the oldest students to teach them about leadership skills and expectations in the family groups. Recommended four times per year.

6. Create a collage, Facebook page, bulletin board or similar media format to capture the family group activities and excitement throughout the year.

Special Connection with Peyton Manning Children's Hospital

Who wore number 18 on the Indianapolis Colts team? Of course, Peyton Manning, quarterback for the Indianapolis Colts, who led the team to a Super Bowl Championship in 2007!

During Peyton Manning's career in Indianapolis, he also became highly involved in the Peyton Manning Children's Hospital on the north side of the city. He visited the children there and often shot commercials and service announcements from the hospital.

The students at St. Louis de Montfort Catholic School in Fishers, Indiana, viewed Peyton Manning as a role model and wanted to help at the hospital that was his namesake. The student council organized two simple events that clearly connected the children at Peyton Manning Children's Hospital and the students at St. Louis de Montfort Catholic School.

First, the entire student body participated in the hospital's Trick or Treat, Off Your Feet Program. Quite simply, the program was based on the fact that the students in the hospital could not trick or treat, so special items were collected for the patients. In October, our student body was quite generous with their donations of crayons, coloring books, markers, cards, puzzles and simple board games and craft kits.

Before Halloween, the student council representatives and moderators delivered the items to the hospital. Some ill children were able to receive the gifts directly from our students as the entire delivery and all interactions were videotaped. Of course, for the school student body, the highlight was watching the videos of students and children in the hospital working on puzzles or crafts or playing cards together. What a touching video! I (Annette) strongly encourage schools to organize this simple event for your school in conjunction with a local children's hospital.

The second project was a "coin war" as signaled by the four large tubs that were placed in the hallway. The grades were paired (Grades 8 and 1, Grades 7 and 2, Grades 6 and 3, Grades 4 and 5) and had the goal of placing the most amount of money in their respective tubs. Preschoolers and kindergarteners could place money in any tub. The idea was that silver counted toward the final amount, and pennies were deducted from the final amount. Of course, the older students taught the younger students to place silver in their tub and pennies in other tubs! What a game of strategy and collaboration!

At the end of the week, the student council representatives tabulated the results and announced the grand winners to the school. The winning grade levels enjoyed a pizza party together. Following Catholic School Week, the student council leaders presented a check, collected from the school-wide and community participation, to a representative of Peyton Manning Children's Hospital during a school-wide Mass. The representative often shared touching remarks and stories about the children in the hospital and explained the direct impact that our students' continuous interactions and contributions had made.

Our school community enjoyed participating in the Trick or Treat, Off Your Feet Program and the Annual Coin War. Every September, students would ask about the annual Coin War and collection for the children in the hospital and share their plans to donate their favorite crayons or coloring books. These programs taught our children so much about generosity, kindness and gratitude for their health. Most importantly, our hearts and prayers were focused on the ill children and their families.

Pathway for Trick or Treat, Off Your Feet Program

1. Communicate with the hospital representative about the types of donations needed.

2. Communicate information about the Trick or Treat, Off Your Feet Program with the parents and stakeholders. Information should include the purpose of the program, list of items for donation, the timeframe for collection and the collection sites.

3. Meet with student council members to discuss the list of needed items for the children in the hospital.

4. Develop a list of talking points, so all student council members feel comfortable explaining the reason for the collection to their classmates.

5. Place collection boxes throughout the school and in the back of church for about three weeks.

6. Organize donations in a presentable manner. We used small colorful plastic baskets with handles accented with tissue paper and ribbon.

7. Communicate with the hospital representative to determine the delivery date, time and number of students permitted for the delivery.

8. Videotape the delivery and interactions between the students and children in the hospital. Show the video to the entire student body!

Pathway for the Coin War for Peyton Manning Children's Hospital

1. Communicate with the hospital representative about the school's annual Coin War during Catholic Schools Week.

2. Communicate information about the Coin War with the parents and stakeholders. Information should include the purpose of the program, rules for the Coin War, the timeframe for collection and the collection site. The winning grade level pair will receive a pizza party!

3. Develop a list of talking points, so all members feel comfortable explaining the Coin War purpose and rules to their classmates.

4. Place collection tubs, labeled with grade pairs, near the school office during Catholic Schools Week.

5. Count the coins and determine the grade pair winners! The winners are announced at the end of the day on Friday.

6. Invite the hospital representative to Mass the following week.

7. Prepare a speech and present the check to the hospital representative.

8. Order pizza for the winning grade level pairs.

The Tradition of the St. Theodore Guerin Award

Traditions are one of the best aspects of Catholic schools. At St. Louis de Montfort Catholic School in Fishers, Indiana, the teachers and staff members engage in a special tradition during the first week of January. Using a special rubric, they nominate a Teacher of the Year, which is appropriately known as the St. Theodore Guerin Award, named after the only Catholic saint from Indiana.

The nominations are returned to the principal, who tabulates the results to determine the St. Theodore Guerin Awardee. He or she is recognized following the all-school Catholic Schools Week liturgy. For the ceremony, the previous year's recipient creates the script, delivers the presentation and presents flowers and an angel to the awardee. The principal secretly invites the family members of the St. Theodore Guerin Awardee to the liturgy and award ceremony.

Perhaps your school community would like to replicate this idea as part of the Catholic Schools Week celebration. Below, I (Annette) have included the rubric, background about St. Theodore Guerin, and remarks at the special presentation honoring the 2016 recipient, Mrs. Jennifer Popovich, second grade teacher.

Rubric for St. Theodore Guerin Award

Rate the following criteria under each theme between 1 and 5.

1= satisfactory

2= very good

3= commendable

4= outstanding

5= exemplary

Faith and Dedication

Committed to teaching in Catholic schools as evidenced by their faith and service.

Always looking for a Catholic teachable moment.

Brings God into his or her perception of students' growth.

Shares faith through words and actions with students, staff members and school community.

Relator and Student Rapport

Able to achieve important attitude outcomes with students.

Engages in significant relationships with students, family, colleagues and community members.

Extends time with students to show interest in non-academic activities.

Helps students understand their faith through caring, compassion and effective communication.

Developer and Motivator

Able to stretch students to their highest potential.

Finds something special in each student and highlights his or her talents and interests.

Is flexible to meet individual needs of students.

Provides humor to engage and motivate students.

Empathy

Aware of how personal feelings and experiences impact students' lives.

Cares and recognizes students' happiness and success.

Helps students feel that their ideas and contributions are significant.

Cares about difficulties encountered by students and their families.

Responsible and Professional

Works to improve instruction and school-wide initiatives and programs.

Shares educational philosophy and best practices with other educators.

Engages in shared leadership and essential leadership roles in the school community.

Is seen as "going above and beyond" as a teacher leader.

St. Theodore Guerin Background

During Catholic Schools Week, the St. Theodore Guerin Award is presented to a faculty member who is nominated by his or her colleagues and best exemplifies the qualities of this saint. This is the seventh presentation of the award, named in honor of Indiana's St. Theodore Guerin, at St. Louis de Montfort Catholic School.

Theodore Guerin was a French nun who left France in 1840 with five companions for the wild forest of a territory known as Indiana. The sisters settled just a few miles northwest of Terre Haute and lived in humble surroundings. They established a motherhouse for the Sisters of Providence, who cared for the sick and the poor. In addition, they educated the children of pioneer families in the area. It was very difficult for Saint Theodore to live in Indiana as there was always a lack of food, the cabins were tiny, and the weather was very cold. She placed her faith and trust in God. Within a year, in July 1841, the sisters opened St. Mary's Academy for Young Ladies. Today, this school is known as Saint Mary of the Woods College.

The Blessed Mother Theodore Guerin was recognized as a saint by Pope Benedict XVI on October 15, 2006. This saint put God first in her life. She overcame challenges through love, prayer, trust and good works. She has been called a visionary, a model of virtue and a source of inspiration and hope. Through her strength, challenges and humility, St. Theodore Guerin serves as an exemplary role model for all Catholic educators.

Presentation to St. Theodore Guerin Recipient, Mrs. Jennifer Popovich

"Blessed Theodore Guerin was a determined, compassionate and hard-working woman. She put the needs of others before her own. These are the traits found in the teacher receiving the St. Theodore Guerin Award today.

I have had the pleasure of working with this teacher for four years. She goes above and beyond to provide the best education she can for her students. She finds innovative ways to serve each child individually, not only with the curriculum, but also to be the best follower of Jesus that can be. She works hard every single day to make sure that all the students are given exactly what they need.

Others who work with her have told me that they witnessed her love of teaching and her love for students. She truly has a gift of being able to instruct the children in a way that keeps them engaged and eager to learn. She works many hours outside the school day to prepare new lessons. She also has a sincere ability to show compassion and care to all her students. She makes each individual student feel special and important.

Past students used the following adjectives to describe her: smart, polite, outstanding, caring, loving and friendly. Students also commented that she must love Coke because she is always drinking it! My favorite quote that sums up this wonderful teacher came from a current student who said, "I love coming to school because I get to see Mrs. Popovich in the morning, and she always gives me the biggest hugs!"

Jennifer is truly Christ to her students. It is a pleasure to witness her enthusiasm as she prepares the class to receive two beautiful sacraments of First Reconciliation and First Communion. The strength of her own faith is evident each and every day by how she develops her children's understanding of God's love and deepens their faith and love for Him.

Jennifer Popovich is a true leader at St. Louis de Montfort Catholic School. She exhibits the strong qualities of St. Theodore Guerin every day through her words and actions. It is my honor to present the St. Theodore Guerin Award to Mrs. Jennifer Popovich."

Congratulations to Mrs. Jennifer Popovich! I am looking forward to learning who will receive future St. Theodore Guerin Awards.

Pathway for the Creation of the St. Theodore Guerin Award:

1. Explain award to staff, students, parents, parish community, community (fall)

2. Distribute nomination form to teachers and staff (December)

3. Collect nomination forms and tally results (December)

4. Contact the recipient's family (December/January)

5. Write speech for recipient (December/January) (One school's tradition is for the previous year's awardee to write the speech and present the award to the recipient.)

Last Day of School Tradition: Prayer Service

For 180 days, we, as the teachers, staff members and administrators, have been modeling and providing a loving and caring Catholic community for the children entrusted to our care. With the students as the center of our attention, our efforts have been focused on growing their faith, realizing their potential and developing their leadership skills. Academically, we have celebrated their successes and supported them during their challenges throughout the year. We have worked on forming their social development—how to be a good friend, how to apologize, how to win gracefully, how to make mistakes, and how to laugh and have fun! With Christ as the foundation, we have taught that our community is family.

Because our eighth grade students have graduated, the seventh grade students have their first official leadership role of leading the prayer service on the last day of school. The seventh grade students plan the uplifting music, readings and prayers of the faithful. My favorite part of the prayer service is the special blessing for those students and teachers who are leaving the school community. Before the closing song, any student or teacher who is leaving the school community stands as each person in the student body and staff extends his or her hand over them for the Irish blessing:

May the road rise up to meet you.
May the wind be always at your back.
May the sun shine warm upon your face,
The rain fall soft upon your fields,
And until we meet again,
May God hold you in the palm of his hand.

Pathway for Last Day of School Tradition: Prayer Service

1. Meet with seventh grade students about the prayer service in January.

2. Discuss leadership responsibility, songs, readings and Irish blessing with them.

3. Invite parents and stakeholders to prayer service.

4. Gather students and staff in church for prayer service.

5. Praise the seventh grade students following their first official leadership responsibility.

CHAPTER 7
Academic Events for Community Engagement

Back-to-School Night

Back-to-School Nights are generally the first occasion when parents will be gathered as a captive audience to learn about the school. Given the significance of this event, Back-to-School Nights should be well-advertised at least three months in advance. I would recommend sharing the Back-to-School information (date, time, location, length of meeting, babysitting availability) in the late spring, early summer, mid-summer, and late summer via the school publications and social media outlets.

Back-to-School meetings can have various formats and styles. My preference is two evenings, one evening grades 5 through 8 and the other evening pre-kindergarten through fourth grade. Be sure to check local high school calendars to avoid conflicts with the high school orientation evenings. As a professional staff, the special area teachers, who attend both evenings, integrated their presentations into the grade level meetings. Instructional assistants were strongly encouraged to attend and share information with the parents as well.

For each Back-to-School event, the parents and staff members gathered in the cafeteria or auditorium. The pastor opened the meeting with prayer and shared his perspective on education. He often focused on the partnership between the school personnel and parents in guiding the children in spiritual and education formation. The pastor's remarks set the tone for the meeting, so communicate clearly about his message and delivery to the audience.

The administrator would introduce each teacher, special area teacher and staff member who is affiliated with the school. Following introductions, school staff members would depart the meeting to finish last-minute preparations prior to the parents' arrival at the classrooms.

Then, the administrator would continue with a PowerPoint presentation focused on the progress and goals of the school related to the areas of Catholic mission, leadership and governance, academic excellence and operational vitality. The school goals should be in alignment with the pastor and the School Commission or Board. Other school news should be conveyed, such as an application for a National Blue Ribbon, the completion of master's degrees and presentations on the local, state or national levels, delivered by the highly-qualified, professional educators. The third section should focus on students' safety, sharing information about regular safety drills, familiarity with the National Sex Offender Registry and expectation of volunteers to complete VIRTUS (or a similar program) prior to volunteering at the school.

Effective communication is an essential ingredient to a high-performing school. During the Back-to-School presentation, share the school's communication plan with the parents. Parents should know the communication process and frequency for an emergency, emails, newsletters, grading system, phone calls and in-person conferences. Throughout the school year, share updates on the school goals mentioned at Back-to-School Night.

After the administrator's presentation, the parents are invited to attend a break-out session with the teacher. My recommendation is scheduling two 45-minute sessions, so parents have the opportunity to visit at least two teachers during the evening. Teachers should be thoroughly prepared with a formal presentation using technology and/or handouts. The teachers' presentations must be rehearsed—no off-the-cuff talking!

As much as parents are anticipating more knowledge about their children's curriculum and classroom procedures, parents really want to feel that their children are safe with a warm and caring teacher who is professional and competent with a sense of humor.

Pathways to Back-to-School Night

1. Create a communication plan for parents (example: newsletters, social media, emergencies).

2. Share information about Back-to-School Nights with parents, teachers, staff members (dates, times, length of meetings, format, schedule, babysitting availability).

3. Check local high school orientation events and Back-to-School Nights to avoid conflicts.

4. Communicate expectations for attendance, presentation format and types of handouts to teachers and staff members.

5. Prepare opening prayer.

6. Prepare PowerPoint presentation and remarks.

7. Communicate with pastor about opening remarks.

8. Prepare introduction list and fun fact about the teachers and staff members.

Grandparents Day Program (or Special Person Day Program)

In autumn, one special tradition is Grandparents Day or Special Person Day. Given that some students' grandparents may not live nearby or are too ill to travel, we expanded Grandparents Day to include a special person so that all students felt included in the festivities. The principal selected a small team of teachers, staff members, parents and students to assist with plans and logistics for the event. The goal of the committee was to plan a simple and short event, meaning a half day or less, that was meaningful to the students, grandparents and special guests. After numerous configurations, the preferred schedule was starting at noon and ending at dismissal at 3:00 p.m. Grandparents appreciate having the morning to travel and the weekend to spend with their grandchildren.

After the day and time was selected, the students on the committee designed an invitation for the event. Students personalized the invitations by drawing, coloring and writing a special message for their grandparents or special guests.

Based on experience, my school community preferred this schedule:

- 12:00-1:00 p.m. Mass

- 1:00-1:15 p.m. Move to school

- 1:15-2:45 p.m. Activities (Rotation by last name of oldest grandchild)

  Visit classrooms

  Snack and refreshments in cafeteria

  Photo opportunity

- 2:45-3:00 p.m. Prepare for dismissal

Keep in mind that grandparents and special guests may need extra travel time or use of an elevator. Simple treats like cookies and lemonade are easy to serve and require minimal prep and clean-up. Enlist a parent team to volunteer to assist with each rotation area. Also, students will need signed permission slips from their parents or guardians in order to leave with their grandparents or special guests.

Pathway to Grandparents Day Program (or Special Person Program)

1. Select a Grandparents Day / Special Person Day Program Committee.

2. Decide the date and time for the event.

3. Design the invitation for the event.

4. Plan the master schedule for the event.

5. Prepare permission slips for change in transportation.

6. Distribute permission slips to students.

7. Track permission slips and communicate permission with teachers.

8. Secure teams of parent volunteers to assist with each rotation.

International Fair

Every other year, the students in grades 5 through 8 participate in the International Fair. (The Science Fair occurs in the alternating year. For example, a fifth grader would work on the International Fair in grades 5 and 7 and the Science Fair in grades 6 and 8.) The principal assists the teachers with forming a committee of teachers, parents and students. The teachers in grades 5 through 8 determine the criteria and expectations for the requirements of the project for each grade level. The requirements, especially in English and social studies, become more specific, detailed and require higher level thinking skills as the students progress through the grade levels.

For simplicity, the pairs of students were assigned a country, keeping the country's information, traditions and level of difficulty in mind. For example, our school used this general guideline for assigning the countries to the students:

- Grade 5: Europe

- Grade 6: Central and South America

- Grade 7: Africa

- Grade 8: Asia

Typically, for the social studies requirement, all students would create a poster, dress in costume and provide maps, artifacts and flags of the country. The students did not create food samples representing their countries because of concern for possible allergic reactions and building cleanliness. The English requirement included a research paper about the country and an artistic or musical contribution of the country. Again, the expectations for higher level thinking and problem-solving increase as the student moves from 5th to 8th grade. Throughout the process, from introducing the project to the International Fair, teachers should guide and monitor students' timeline and progress, ensuring that students are progressing and completing the requirements in a timely manner.

Prior to the International Fair, the committee chair should invite parents to decorate the gym and create a layout for the tables by continent. Teachers should schedule a time to tour the International Fair with their students. For students in grades 2 through 4, the International Fair committee designed a "passport" as students toured and asked questions of the older students. The International Fair has been a fabulous addition to our school traditions as it reinforced our school values of respect and tolerance for all nationalities.

Pathway for the International Fair

1. Create an International Fair committee.

2. Determine the grade level requirements for the project.

3. Assign a country to each student or pair of students.

4. Share the project requirements with the students.

5. Ask parents to decorate and plan the gym layout by continent.

6. Invite teachers to schedule a time to tour the International Fair.

7. Invite parents and community members to tour the International Fair.

8. Design and distribute a passport for students in grades 2, 3, and 4.

CHAPTER 8
Special Events for Community Engagement

Mentoring Program for New Parents

Sharing the school's special traditions and cultural norms with new parents goes a long way in creating a vibrant school community. One highly successful program at my school was the mentoring program for new parents. For the most part, I (Annette) would rely on my strong relationships with parents to assist with the foundational plan of the program. As I developed relationships with parents, I would keep a master list of the highly engaged and supportive parents who I thought would serve as excellent mentors for our new families. In addition, I would note the grade level and gender of their children.

In September, I would reach out to the highly engaged parents and invite them to participate in the mentoring program for new parents. As soon as the registration process began, I would start the process of matching the mentor parents with the new parents. Since children are the focal point of the school, I would use the grade level and gender of the children to match the families. As expected, sometimes I would need additional mentors in a particular grade level. In this case, I would reach out to the current families in that grade level and ask for volunteers for the mentor program.

The Mentoring Program for New Families consisted of three sections, including connection, information and relationships.

Connection

In late February, I would form a small committee of three or four mentor parents. With the assistance of this committee, we would identify five touch points, meaning conversations or interactions, with the new families. One touchpoint would occur during the summer so the mentor families and new families could meet in person. The second touchpoint, occurring about four to five weeks into the school year, is highly strategic as this timeframe is when many new parents have questions and are anticipating parent-teacher conferences. The third touchpoint is scheduled in early December between Thanksgiving and Christmas.

Once the second semester is in full gear, we schedule a touchpoint in mid-February and a final touchpoint in mid-May. Overall, the goal is to maintain consistent and supportive contact with the new families in the beginning of the year, then gradually let the scheduled contacts decrease. Hopefully, the new family will feel comfortable reaching out to the mentor family as needed.

Information

Next, we would design or update the information portion of the program. We would create an outline of topics and timeline for discussion with all new families. It is essential that all new families receive a consistent and timely messages regarding important information related to the school environment. For example, relevant information should include key points from the family/parent school handbook, communication from and with school personnel, spiritual events, academics, special traditions, fundraisers and special programs, such as Back-to-School Night or the Trick or Treat, Off Your Feet Program.

Relationships

Mentor parents should reach out with a phone call to the new parents. The first call should include an invitation to meet at a park or for an ice cream treat. The goal is to build a relationship with the new family, so the new parents will feel comfortable with asking questions and joining the school community. By following the timeline, mentor parents should share upcoming events and invite new parents to attend these events or become involved in school activities.

Each mentor family should receive a master list of upcoming school activities, events and programs. In order to direct the new family to interesting and appropriate programs, the mentor family should engage in conversation about the new family's interests and talents. At the end of the year, the new parents should receive a survey about the Mentoring Program for New Families. Remember to solicit feedback from the mentor families as well.

Pathway to a Successful Mentoring Program for New Parents

1. Build collaborative relationships with parents.

2. Create a master list of highly-engaged parents.

3. Use grade level and gender of children to match families.

4. Request additional volunteers if needed.

5. Form a small committee of mentor parents.

6. Create a timeline of touchpoints with new families.

7. Create a list of important information for the mentoring program.

8. Distribute a monthly list of school and parish programs and events.

9. Request that new families complete a survey at the end of the year.

10. Solicit feedback about the mentoring program from the mentor families.

Family Fun: Math Nights

Join the fun! Many schools offer opportunities for families to gather for an enjoyable dinner and academic night. I recommend scheduling Family Fun Math Nights once each semester, preferably early fall and late winter, and inviting students in kindergarten through second grade to attend with their families. Keep in mind that Family Fun Math Nights can be scheduled on a staggered schedule or on different nights by grade level in order to minimize the number of students and parents at one time.

Principals or grade level teachers should request an RSVP for the Family Fun Math Night. It is important to know the number of guests for planning the math games and ordering pizza and drinks. For the seating arrangements, parents and students would enjoy sitting in small groups as they can interact with each other during the Family Fun Math Night.

Generally, teachers start the evening with dinner, pizza and drinks, then move to the math portion of the evening. For the math activity, be creative and use technology wherever possible. Teachers should plan a variety of leveled math activities that involve problem-solving and interacting among the students and parents. At the end of the evening, teachers should distribute participation ribbons to each student. Thank the parents for their time, support and participation in Family Fun Math Night.

Pathway to Family Fun: Math Nights

1. Schedule the Family Fun Nights.

2. Communicate the schedule and invited grade levels.

3. Ask parents to RSVP in order to plan for pizza and drinks.

4. Plan seating arrangements to facilitate small group interaction.

5. Start the evening with dinner (pizza and drinks).

6. Plan a variety of leveled math activities.

7. Distribute ribbons to each participating child.

8. Thank parents for their participation and support

Veterans Day

Veterans Day is one of my favorite community events at St. Louis de Montfort Catholic School. In the school's inaugural year in 2000, the first Veterans Day program was simple and was celebrated around the flagpole with fewer than 150 students. Eight years later, the program was moved to the gym, where over 475 students honored our country's current service men and women and veterans with an extensive program and patriotic reception.

Pathways for a Veterans Day Observance

1. Create a committee of staff members and parents.

2. Send invitations to parents and parishioners.

3. Share the date, time and agenda with the local Chamber of Commerce.

4. Encourage service men and women to wear their uniforms if they would like.

5. Request photos (not originals) from students and staff members of their family's service men and women. Ask for the name of the person in the photo, their connection to the school (for example, Mary Smith's grandfather), their branch of service and years served.

6. Create a photo collage with their information at the entry of the school.

7. Create a scrolling PowerPoint with the photos and their information to use during the program.

8. Teach students three to four patriotic songs and the service hymns of each branch of the military (Air Force, Army, Navy, Coast Guard).

9. Hang flags of each branch of the military in the gym.

10. Ask a local veteran to prepare a short presentation for the students and community.

11. Engage all students through a writing activity: "What Freedom Means to Me."

12. Plan a patriotic reception with special décor, thank you notes, snacks and refreshments. Hold the reception near the gym (less walking for veterans) and have plenty of seating.

13. Sample Agenda

- Opening prayer

- Pledge of Allegiance

- National Anthem

- Remarks from selected speaker

- Patriotic song

- Select three-five students to read essays, "What Freedom Means to Me."

- Students sing service hymns. Please ask veterans and current military personnel to stand to be recognized when their service hymn is sung.

- Closing remarks

- Patriotic song

- Take a photo of service men and women in attendance.

- Patriotic reception

CHAPTER 9
Thinking Outside the Box

Fishers (IN) Chamber of Commerce: Business of the Year Award

In the world of school competition for students, Catholic school leaders may need to think and look outside the box for ways to promote their schools. On numerous occasions, I (Annette) have heard Catholic school principals explain that their primary objectives are to share and model the faith to students and the school community and to provide a solid academic foundation for the students. Of course, I strongly agree with both points. However, I must also add a third point. As Catholic school principals, we truly run a business, which involves budget and finance knowledge, marketing skills, advance and development plans, and human resource competencies.

During my eight years as principal at St. Louis de Montfort Catholic School in Fishers, Indiana, I recognized that the school was in somewhat of a transient state with professional parents often relocating in and out of the neighborhoods surrounding the school. Each year, I deliberately increased my efforts in the business aspect of the role of principal, realizing that marketing, budgeting and development plans were critical to the viability and sustainability of this suburban Catholic school.

One afternoon, an intriguing message via email was sent to me. The town of Fishers had opened the site to submit applications for Fishers Business of the Year. Immediately, I saw possibilities and opportunities! Our school could be recognized in the local community as a school of excellence—and as a business. Our school personnel could interact with other businesses to investigate potential partnerships. Our school could be formally recognized as a thriving and integral part of the community of Fishers.

Without hesitation, I completed the application and mailed it to the Fishers Chamber of Commerce. One important point stuck with me: How does your school engage with the community? This question was on our application, and I was able to cite confidently our service to the community via the St Louis de Montfort Food Pantry and special grade level service projects that benefited various organizations in the Fishers community. In addition, the school's hot lunch program was organized and provided through local restaurants. The application process confirmed that St. Louis de Montfort Catholic School was truly an integral part of the community.

The Fishers Chamber of Commerce agreed with our application, especially with the aspect of community outreach. St. Louis de Montfort Catholic School was presented with a plaque in the category of Business of the Year as the school principal and two guests were invited to a special luncheon honoring the top three finalists. I was so excited just for the school to be recognized as one of the top three finalists for the Fishers Chamber of Commerce Business of the Year. The representatives shared that we needed to produce a two to three minute video about our school to show at the luncheon.

In this video the students, teachers and parents were the stars. We spelled ST LOUIS DE MONTFORT CATHOLIC SCHOOL and shared a word and sentence that represented our school. For example, for S: "Students are the heart of your school!" T: "Teachers are dedicated and caring professional educators." The video was fantastic as students, teachers and parents all gave their input into creating sentences that corresponded with each letter.

At the luncheon, the Fishers Chamber of Commerce announced the top three finalists for Business of the Year and played our videos. I must say that our school video was endearing and captured the hearts of those in the room. After the video, the Fishers Business of the Year was announced as St. Louis de Montfort Catholic School. I walked to the podium and thanked the SLDM school community and the Fishers Chamber of Commerce. Then I realized that I needed to introduce myself as the principal since I was not part of the video—only the director!

What a fantastic accolade that was shared by the entire community. Our school continued its involvement in the local Fishers community, and we enjoyed the additional recognition as a vibrant school that was highly engaged and cared about the Fishers community.

Pathway to View Your School as a Business

Community Awards

1. Investigate local community recognition programs, such as Chamber of Commerce Awards.

2. Learn about the awards and the application process.

3. Name a committee to assist with the application process, if needed.

4. Be prepared to share your "school's resume," meaning your school's accomplishments. Toot your horn!

5. Be prepared to provide supplemental materials, such as videos, marketing materials, testimonials, etc.

6. Keep the spotlight on the students, staff and community members, not administrators or superintendent.

Marketing Internally

1. How do teachers and staff members market the school? (Yes, marketing is everyone's job!)

2. Does your school have a communication plan for current parents?

3. Does your school have a marketing plan for prospective parents?

4. Does your school keep a record and follow-up with all prospective parents who take a tour of the school?

5. Does your school engage actively in social media?

6. Does your school have personal contacts with local newspapers and media?

7. Does your school have a process of exit interviews for students and parents who are leaving your school?

Marketing Externally

1. How does your school engage with the community?

2. Is there a local Business of the Year application? If so, apply!

3. Create a list of local community groups and list how your school impacts, touches or affects each group

4. If you see holes in the list, then fill them. Eliminate duplicates.

5. How well is your school known in the local community?

6. What activities and service projects does your school lead or coordinate in the community?

7. Can your school and parish sponsor an event for the community such as a 5K or fall festival?

8. Do you invite prospective parents to your Christmas concert?

9. How is your school connected on a national level and international arena? (For example, does your school hold memberships in national organizations, such as National Catholic Educational Association? Have your teachers connected with another educator in a different country via Skype or email?

Budget and Finance

1. Is the principal involved in all aspects of the school budget?

2. Does the principal receive monthly updates from the business office?

3. Is there a designated system or company for tuition collection?

4. Is there a designated system or company for tuition assistance?

5. Is the school involved in promoting school choice, vouchers or tax credit/scholarship programs?

6. Does the school have an annual fundraiser to supplement the needs of the school (not an annual contribution to operating expenses in the school budget)?

7. Does your school budget reflect your Catholic mission?

Advancement and Development

1. Does your school have a three to five year strategic plan?

2. Does your school track potential students from the parish database?

3. How does your school engage with alumni?

4. How does your school engage with grandparents and other friends of the school?

5. Have you formed a specialized team to assist with advancement and development of the school?

6. Does your school have a plan for capital campaigns, endowments and other long-range financial contributions?

7. Does your school have a facilities plan?

8. Is there a financial plan for long-term professional development for the teachers and staff members?

Human Resources

1. How do you effectively advertise for open positions in your school?

2. Do you have a list of legal, appropriate and job-related questions for the interview?

3. How do teachers participate in the interview process?

4. Do you always check multiple references?

5. Do you have a mentor program for all new teachers and new-to-your-school teachers?

6. Do you have a training program for new staff members, substitute teachers and volunteers?

7. What is the evaluation process for teachers and staff members? Has the evaluation process been shared with all teachers and staff members?

8. What is the process to address underperformance in your school?

9. How do you handle misunderstandings and conflict in your school?

10. Is your faculty handbook updated annually?

CHAPTER 10
Retention Leads to Recruitment

What is the connection between retention and recruitment? Retention means families choose to enroll in the school for another year. Recruitment is the process of actively persuading a new family to enroll in the school.

Retention of currently enrolled families is a critical component of the school marketing and enrollment plan. Many of our parents of currently enrolled students volunteer and are involved in establishing or continuing our meaningful school traditions. Parent volunteers are invaluable with planning events, sharing the spiritual and/or educational purpose of the event, communicating the details about the event to other parents and being fully engaged with the event.

Word of mouth is most effective for sharing the good news and special traditions about our schools. Ultimately, our parent volunteers will be the best ambassadors of our school!

CHAPTER 11
Attitude of Gratitude

Thank you! Thank you! Thank you! Effective Catholic school leaders model and practice an "attitude of gratitude." Most principals recognize that effective schools require an extensive network of skilled leaders and volunteers to support the mission and vision of our Catholic schools. Teachers, staff members, pastors, board members, parishioners and community members are vital to the success and advancement of our Catholic schools. We must not take their support for granted. Remember to show appreciation and to say thank you!

Depending on the situation, determine if a private or public thank you is more appropriate. For a private thank you, keep a stockpile of thank you notes and prayer cards in your office. As a routine, I (Annette) wrote one thank you note each morning and kept a list of people who received a card from me. If I wrote a thank you to the student, I mailed the card to the parents. Public expressions of thanks were announced to the student body over the public address system or during a general assembly. In addition, special public thank you gestures, often accompanied by ceramic angels, flowers or planters, were given to outgoing teachers, staff members, or board members.

To show appreciation to parents, call each family at least once during the school year. The point of the conversation is to listen and to thank the parents for sending their children to your school. Inquire about the children and ask how the year is progressing. During the conversation, assure parents that you are accessible should they have any further questions, concerns or ideas. For Catholic Schools Week, ensure that each family receives a handwritten thank you note from the principal.

All teachers should send postcards to welcome and appreciate the students at the beginning of the year. In addition, follow-up phone calls from teachers between the start of the school year and parent-teacher conferences are much appreciated by parents!

Our thoughtfulness and appreciation to others yields tremendous dividends in building and sustaining relationships in a Catholic school community.

Pathway for an Attitude of Gratitude

Administrators

1. Call all parents at least once during the school year. The point of the conversation is to listen, inquire about their children and ask how the school year is progressing. Thank parents for sending their children to the school. Assure parents that you are accessible to continue the conversation or to answer any questions—on the phone, via email or in person.

2. Ensure that each parent receives a handwritten thank you note from you during Catholic Schools Week.

3. Write one thank you note daily, keeping a list of the recipients.

4. Deliver birthday cards (and a thank you) to teachers and staff members.

5. Write thank you notes to parent volunteers.

6. Participate in an Attitude of Gratitude by verbally thanking students, colleagues, pastors, parents and community members.

7. Treat staff members to a catered lunch or sundae bar.

8. Establish a public thank you tradition for outgoing teachers, staff members and board members.

Teachers and Staff Members

1. Send postcards to welcome students prior to the start of the school year.

2. Call parents between Back-to-School Night and parent-teacher conferences.

3. Send thank you notes promptly to parent volunteers.

4. Send thank you cards promptly for Christmas gifts.

5. Participate in an Attitude of Gratitude by verbally thanking students, colleagues, pastors and administrators.

CHAPTER 12
How Do I Do All This?

Simply stated, it is impossible for a principal to successfully brand and market a school and recruit and retain students alone. Though marketing must be a high priority on the principal's endless to-do list, it cannot be solely his or her responsibility. So, where can help be found?

Develop a Marketing Committee

A common school governance model calls for a school advisory board. In many dioceses, this body is composed of a select group of parents, usually chosen by the pastor and principal, to provide a voice in discussions of policy and school direction. This group can do much more than attend a monthly meeting. Committees are a powerful way to extend the reach of a council and to support the principal's work. Select a person on your council to be the chair of the Marketing Committee. That person would be tasked with recruiting other parents to help on the committee, which would then work to set and reach marketing goals and targets, seek direction from the principal in frequent one-on-one meetings and make monthly reports to the full council on the progress achieved. The principal must be involved to set targets, to share his or her vision, to facilitate resources and to inject enthusiasm into the work. Letting go of some of the hands-on work requires trust and isn't always easy, especially in a small school environment, but it is the only way to put in the necessary time to fully form a marketing strategy.

Who?

Who could be on this committee? Look deep into your parent talent pool and ask people to share their gifts. Many schools conduct an annual "time and talent" survey. This could be as simple as sending out a Google form to your parent community asking about interest in volunteering at the school and about their career field and hobbies. You may discover that parents are involved in marketing, or run small businesses, or have IT skills, or are artists or video producers. Using that information to select people to approach to serve on the committee is a great strategy. Your current parents are at your school because they believe in your mission and because they support your work. Most parents will be flattered to be asked to get involved. One of the most common reasons that people do not volunteer themselves is because they are not asked to do so. People can be humble—they may not consider their gifts as being in demand and therefore may not even think of approaching the school themselves. A little bit of strategy can go a long way.

Pathway to Sharing the Work

1. Identify your marketing plan goals. What do you currently have in place? What would you like to have? What is your enrollment target?

2. Identify one parent leader to be your Marketing Chairperson. The parent should be dependable, available and organized. This person can usually be found volunteering for other activities in the school, such as your school advisory council.

3. If you have not yet done so, conduct a short time and talent survey. Identify parents who have skills that could support your marketing goals.

4. Work with your chairperson to recruit five to seven parents to be on your Marketing Committee.

5. Meet with the committee to set parameters, focus on targets, brainstorm strategy and schedule meetings.

6. Let the committee get to work!

CONCLUSION

The Book of Proverbs tells us to "Train the young in the way they should go; even when old, they will not swerve from it" (Prov. 22:6). In an increasingly secular world, the formation of children in what is true, beautiful and good has never been more important or more difficult. Few institutions can provide the moral, spiritual and academic foundation that a Catholic school can. But, all too often, Catholic schools do not communicate their tremendous impact on the lives of children and families. Now, more than ever before, Catholic schools need to proudly share their work with the world through effective marketing strategies. If our schools are going to thrive in the future, all principals, pastors, teachers and parents must spread the Good News of Catholic education through new and innovative communication strategies. The work is not always quick or easy, but it, and our Catholic mission, are worth it.

APPENDIX

Appendix A - Archdiocese of Denver Marketing Plan Template Access at:
https://drive.google.com/open?id=1sOfFnG3Aamh5jcZCgHv8GiwLS6kqxdVZQ-5L3RsdF6s

NCEA PUBLICATIONS AND RESOURCES

Burns, E. & Gallagher, G. (2016). *Gather Us In: Admissions, Enrollment, and Retention for Catholic Schools.* Arlington, VA: National Catholic Educational Association.

Cook, T. (2015). *Charism and Culture: Cultivating Catholic Identity In Catholic Schools.* Arlington, VA: National Catholic Educational Association.

Jones, A. & Gallagher, G. (2016). *Best Practices of National Blue Ribbon Schools: A Collection from Distinguished Catholic Schools.* Arlington, VA: National Catholic Educational Association.

Ozar, L. (2012). *National Standards and Benchmarks for Effective Catholic Elementary and Secondary Schools.* Chicago: Loyola University.

Quinn, E.W. (2005). *It's a Catholic School...Let's Keep It Catholic.* Arlington, VA: National Catholic Educational Association

ABOUT THE AUTHORS

Adam J. Dufault is currently the Interim Superintendent of Catholic Schools in the Archdiocese of Denver. He previously served as a teacher and a principal in the Archdiocese of Chicago for 14 years.

Annette Marie Jones, Ed.S, works currently as the Assistant Director of Leadership Development at the National Catholic Educational Association in Arlington, Virginia. She has previously served as a teacher, assistant principal and principal in the Archdiocese of Indianapolis and Diocese of Lafayette-in-Indiana for 24 years.